Bible Stories
for
Little Children

Bible Stories
for
Little Children

SOPHIA INSTITUTE PRESS®
Manchester, New Hampshire

Sophia Institute Press®
Box 5284, Manchester, NH 03108
1-800-888-9344
www.sophiainstitute.com

Imprimatur:
John Cardinal McCloskey
Archbishop, New York

Library of Congress Cataloging-in-Publication Data

Bible stories for little children.
   p. cm.
Originally published: [S.l.] : Benziger Brothers, 1882.
ISBN-10: 1-933184-18-3   ISBN-13: 978-1-933184-18-0
(pbk. : alk. paper) 1. Bible stories, English
I. Sophia Institute Press.

BS551.3.B55 2006
220.9'505 — dc22

2006001433

06 07 08 09 10 9 8 7 6 5 4 3 2 1

Contents

The Story of the Old Testament

The Story of the New Testament

Bible Stories
for
Little Children

The Story
of the
Old Testament

The Creation of the World

At one time, dear children, the world in which we live did not exist. There was no land or sea or bright blue sky. There were no trees or plants or flowers. There was no person or thing but God. He always was and always will be.

Then God made the world, the land, and the water; the sun, the moon, and the stars; the birds and the fishes and all the creatures of the earth.

Last of all, God made a man and a woman, whom He named Adam and Eve.

And God is so great and powerful that He made all these in six days, and out of nothing, by His word alone.

On the seventh day God rested from His work and blessed that day. For this reason the Jews kept it holy and called it the *Sabbath,* which means to "rest from labor." But after our blessed Lord was crucified, the Apostles chose Sunday, the first day of the week, as their day of rest, because on that day our Savior rose from the dead.

The Garden of Paradise
The home of Adam and Eve was a lovely garden, in which sweet-smelling flowers and ripe, juicy fruits grew. Pretty birds sang in the branches of the trees, and animals of every kind sported and played together. Everything was peaceful and beautiful.

God told Adam that he and Eve might eat of the fruit of every tree in the garden, except of one, and that one they must not touch.

The First Sin
This was a very little thing to require, and, had our first parents obeyed God, they would have lived forever and would have been happy

---

in this beautiful garden. But one day the Devil tempted Eve to eat the forbidden fruit and told her that if she ate it, she would become as great as God Himself.

Eve was foolish enough to believe this, and in spite of God's command she ate the forbidden fruit.

Then, not satisfied with sinning herself, she coaxed Adam to eat of the fruit also, and in this way sin was brought upon the earth.

Almighty God was angry with Adam and Eve for disobeying Him. To punish them He drove them from the garden and condemned them to spend the rest of their lives in labor and suffering, until they returned to the dust out of which they were made.

This terrible curse was to fall not only on them, but on all who would come after them. But so great is the love of God for His creatures that, even in spite of their sin, God promised that He would send a Redeemer to save mankind.

Cain and Abel .

Adam and Eve had many children. The first two were called Cain and Abel. Cain was a husbandman, or farmer, and Abel was a shepherd. They both offered gifts to God, and as Abel was a good man, his offerings pleased our Lord; but those of Cain, who was wicked, did not please Him. At this, Cain became angry and jealous of his brother, and at last hated him.

One day he asked Abel to go into the fields with him, and while they were there all alone, the wicked Cain killed his brother. Then God cursed Cain for what he had done, and set a mark on him, and Cain went forth a wanderer on the face of the earth.

The Flood

Mankind was now divided into two classes: the good and the wicked.

The first were the descendants of the pious Seth, a child given by God to Adam and Eve to console them for the death of Abel. The wicked were the descendants of the murderer Cain.

After a while the good and the bad married, and, as generally happens in such cases, in time all became wicked.

Then God commanded Noah, who alone remained holy, to build a large boat called an ark, and to go into it with his wife, his three sons, and their wives, and to take with him pairs of every kind of animal.

When this was done, God sent a flood upon the earth. The rain poured from the heavens until the water had risen above the top of the highest mountain.

Every living thing — men, women, and children; beasts, birds, and reptiles — was drowned, except Noah and all that were with him in the ark.

For a whole year the ark floated safely on the waters, at the end of which time it rested on the mountains of Armenia.

Then Noah and his family, and every living thing that was with them, came forth. Once all were out, Noah built an altar and offered sacrifice to God to thank Him for His goodness.

When you are older, you will understand that the ark was a symbol of the Church of God, in which those who seek shelter are safe.

The Tower of Babel

Noah and his three sons, whose names were Sem, Cham, and Japhet, began to cultivate the earth. After a while the number of people on the earth increased, and it was found that all could not live in the same place. Before separating they agreed to build a city with a tower that would reach to heaven, in which they would be safe in case of another flood.

But God punished their pride by changing their language, so that they couldn't understand one another. Before this they had all spoken the same language; now there were many languages. The city and the tower were left unfinished, and the people scattered, going to different parts of the earth.

The Call of Abraham

When Noah had lived 950 years, he died. About a hundred years after his death God

ordered a holy man named Abram, who was
afterward called Abraham, to leave his own
country and go into the land of Canaan. And
God promised Abraham that he would be the
father of a great people, and that in him all
nations would be blessed.

To test him, God at one time told Abraham
to sacrifice his best beloved son, whose name
was Isaac. Abraham hastened to obey, but just
as he was about to kill his son, God sent an

angel to stop him and then gave him a ram to sacrifice instead.

Abraham lived to the age of 175 years and was always the same pious man, ever ready to do the will of God. At his death his son Isaac succeeded him.

Isaac had two sons, Esau and Jacob.

Joseph

Jacob was the father of Joseph and of eleven other sons. Joseph was so good and so obedient that his father loved him better than any of his brothers.

To show his love, Jacob gave Joseph a coat of many colors, and this made his brothers very angry. One day they committed a wicked deed, and when Joseph told his father of it, they hated him all the more.

Some time after, Joseph's father sent him to the field where his brothers were feeding their sheep. When he reached the place, they stripped him of his coat, threw him into a pit, and at last sold him to some merchants who were passing by on their way to Egypt.

Then the brothers dipped Joseph's coat in the blood of a goat and sent it to their father. When the old man saw it, he said, "It is my son's coat. A wild beast has eaten him." And he wept for his beloved boy.

The merchants who bought Joseph took him to Egypt, where, by his piety and wisdom, he soon became a very great man and governor of the land.

The Famine

Nine years after Joseph had been sold, there came a terrible famine, and Jacob sent ten of his sons to Egypt to buy grain. Benjamin, his youngest son, he kept at home, fearing that something would happen to him.

Now, Joseph had charge of the grain in Egypt, and when his brothers came to him, he knew them at once, although they did not know him. He pretended to take them for spies and cast Simeon, one of the oldest, into prison. Then he bade the others go home to their father with the grain they had bought, promising to free Simeon if they would come back with their youngest brother, Benjamin.

The brothers felt that God was now punishing them for their wickedness and went off quite sad. When they reached home, they told everything to their father. At first Jacob refused to let Benjamin go, but when the grain was all eaten up, he was obliged to consent.

The Cup in Benjamin's Sack

The brothers soon reached Egypt and were at once taken to Joseph's palace. Joseph wept for joy when he saw Benjamin and blessed the boy. He asked his brothers to dine with him and waited on them himself.

The next morning their sacks were filled with grain, and they started for home. They had not gone far when a servant came hurrying after them, to say that one of them had stolen a silver cup. To prove that they had not done such a wicked thing, they went back; but when they were searched, the missing cup was found, hidden in Benjamin's sack.

Now, Joseph had ordered one of his servants to place the cup there, so as to try his brothers. When they saw it, they fell at Joseph's feet and offered to be his slaves; but he told them they might all go home, except Benjamin, who would be his slave.

At this, Judah, one of the brothers, begged Joseph to keep him for a slave, and let Benjamin go, saying that their dear old father would die of grief if Benjamin did not return.

Joseph Makes Himself Known

Joseph knew by this that his brothers were no longer the bad men they used to be. When they were alone, Joseph said, "I am Joseph, your brother. Be not afraid. God sent me to Egypt so you might have food when you needed it."

Then he embraced Benjamin and his other brothers, gave them handsome presents, and sent them home to their father.

As soon as Jacob heard that his beloved son was alive, he left for Egypt, taking with him his whole family. Joseph hastened to meet his father and, seeing him, hugged him, weeping.

"Now shall I die with joy," said Jacob, "because I have seen your face." Almost these same words were used, seventeen hundred years afterward, by the holy Simeon, when he saw Jesus presented as a Baby in the Temple.

Joseph gave his father and his brothers land on which to feed their flocks, and they became a great nation. Seventeen years after his arrival in Egypt Jacob died, but Joseph lived to be 110 years old, and he saw his grandchildren before his death.

Joseph's life was, in many ways, like our Savior's. Joseph was hated by his brothers on account of his virtues; Jesus, too, was hated. Joseph was betrayed and sold; so was Jesus. Joseph triumphed in the end and was made governor of Egypt; Jesus was victorious over death and is King of heaven and earth. Joseph saved his brothers from dying of famine; Jesus Christ died to save us from the death of sin.

Moses Is Born

After the death of Joseph, the Hebrews, who were the descendants of Jacob, increased so very fast that the king of Egypt was afraid they would become too powerful. To prevent this he ordered that they should do all the hard work in the country, and, as that might not be enough, he commanded that every baby boy should be drowned as soon as he was born.

About this time, a Hebrew woman had a little boy, whom she loved dearly. She wished to save her baby, so for three months she hid him. When she could hide him no longer, she made a basket of rushes, which she daubed over with slime and pitch so that water could not enter and, with her heart almost breaking, put her baby in it and laid it in the high grass along the river's side. The baby's sister, whose name was Mary, hid nearby to watch.

Shortly after, the king's daughter came down to bathe and, seeing the basket, sent her servant for it. The princess opened it and saw a pretty little boy, and her heart was filled with pity for his poor mother. She decided to save the child and raise him as her son.

The baby's sister now ran up to her and asked if she should find a nurse for him; being told to do so, she brought his mother. The baby was named *Moses,* which means "saved from the water."

Moses' Flight

When Moses was forty years old, he saw an Egyptian beating another Hebrew cruelly. Coming to the defense of the Hebrew, Moses killed the Egyptian, and when other Egyptians heard of it, Moses fled in fear to Midian, in Arabia, where he became a shepherd.

The Burning Bush

One day, while Moses was watching his sheep, God appeared to him in a *burning bush.* Moses was surprised to see that the bush did not burn up, and he went nearer to look at it. God commanded him to stand still and to take off his shoes, as the place was holy.

At the voice of God, Moses fell on his face. Then God told him that he was chosen to free the Hebrews, and for this he must go before the king; but, as he was slow of speech, his brother Aaron would be spokesman.

The Plagues of Egypt

Moses and Aaron went to the Egyptian king and told him that God had ordered him to free the Hebrews. The king not only refused to do this, but even gave the people harder work than before. Moses and Aaron went again to the king, who again refused to do as he was told. So God sent ten plagues on him and his people.

At first the water of the rivers was changed to blood; then frogs covered the whole country; after that the dust of the earth turned into small insects that troubled both man and beast; next came a plague of flies that filled all the houses; and then a disease that killed the cattle. The sixth plague was boils on men and animals; the seventh, a hailstorm that destroyed the grain and fruits; the eighth, a swarm of locusts that ate all the plants the hail had not destroyed; and then a dreadful darkness for three long days.

Before sending the tenth and most terrible plague, God ordered each Hebrew family to sacrifice a lamb on the fourteenth day of the month and to sprinkle the door-posts of each house with its blood.

He commanded them to roast the lamb and eat it with unleavened bread — all of which they did.

That night God's angel visited the houses that were not marked with the blood of the lamb, and there was great mourning among the Egyptians; for in every home, from that of the king down to the poorest man, the oldest child lay dead.

Then the king sent for Moses and Aaron and bade them get out of Egypt as fast as they could, before any more Egyptians would die.

The Passage of the Red Sea

Moses started at once with all his people, but they had not gone many days when the king was sorry that he had let them go and, taking his army, went in pursuit of them.

When the Hebrews, who were on the shores of the Red Sea, saw the army coming, they thought themselves lost, as there seemed no way of escape. But Moses bade them fear not, and when he stretched forth his rod over the sea, as God had commanded him, the waters divided, rising like a wall to the right and the left, leaving a dry passage through which the people crossed over to the other side.

The Egyptians followed, but when Moses again stretched his rod over the sea, the waters rolled back to their place, and the king with his whole army was drowned.

This passage through the Red Sea is a figure of holy Baptism, by which we are freed from the slavery of sin.

Manna in the Desert

When the Hebrews had crossed the Red Sea, they came into a desert, and soon their food was all gone. They could find nothing to eat, but God in His goodness sent a number of quails into their camp and caused a fine bread, called *manna,* to fall from heaven. Later on, when they reached Mount Horeb and had no water, God ordered Moses to strike a rock with his rod, and water at once poured forth in great quantity.

The manna that was sent from heaven to feed the hungry Hebrews, or Israelites, as they were also called, was a figure of the Most Blessed Sacrament, in which our divine Lord gives Himself as food for our souls.

The Ten Commandments

Three months after leaving Egypt the Israelites came to Mount Sinai. Here God called Moses up to the mountain and bade him tell the people that, if they remained faithful to the Lord, He would continue to protect them and would make them a *chosen people.*

God also commanded the people to prepare themselves for two whole days, so as to be ready for the third day. On the morning of the third day it began to thunder and lightning; a thick cloud covered the mountain, and the top of Mount Sinai seemed to be on fire.

Then came the sound of a trumpet, which grew louder and louder until the people trembled with fear. When Moses had led the people to the foot of the mountain, God spoke thus:

*I am the Lord your God. You shall not
    have strange gods before me.
You shall not take the name of the Lord
    your God in vain.
Remember to keep holy the Sabbath day.
Honor your father and mother.*

You shall not kill.

You shall not commit adultery.

You shall not steal.

You shall not bear false witness
against your neighbor.

You shall not covet your neighbor's wife.

You shall not covet your neighbor's goods.

The Israelites, who were trembling with fear, promised to do all that God commanded. Afterward Moses went up to the mountain again and stayed there forty days and forty nights, conversing with God, who gave him two stone tablets on which were written the Ten Commandments.

The Golden Calf

While Moses was living on the mountain, the people began to complain and going to Aaron, asked him to make them gods like those of the Egyptians. Thinking to quiet them, he told them to bring the golden earrings of their wives and daughters. To his great surprise they did. So, being afraid to put them off any longer, Aaron made a golden calf out of the earrings and gave it to the people to worship.

When Moses came down from the mountain and found the people adoring this idol — dancing around it and eating and drinking like pagans — he was so angry that he threw down the stone tablets on which the Commandments were written, and they were broken in their fall. Taking the golden calf, he cast it into the fire and ordered all who continued in idolatry to be put to death. Moses then returned once more to the mountain and begged God to pardon His people. The Lord heard this prayer, and after Moses had made two stone tablets like the first, God wrote the Ten Commandments on them. When Moses came down from the mountain this time, his face shone so brightly that he was obliged to wear a veil, for the people dared not look upon him.

The Twelve Spies

The Israelites stayed a year at Mount Sinai; then they began their march to the Promised Land, and when they had reached its borders, Moses sent twelve men to explore the country. After an absence of forty days they returned, bringing with them some of the fruits of the country. Among these was an enormous bunch of grapes, borne on the shoulders of two men, besides pomegranates and figs. The land, they said, was "flowing with milk and honey," but its people were giants.

At this the Israelites cried out against
Moses and Aaron for bringing them out of
Egypt. To punish them the Lord declared
that they should wander for forty years in the
desert, and that not one of them who was over
twenty-one years of age should ever enter into
the Promised Land.

The Sin of Moses

The last year that the Israelites were in the
desert, they encamped at a place where there
was no water. God told Moses to strike a rock
with his rod. Moses hesitated for a moment;
then he struck the rock, and water at once
gushed forth. For his doubt of God's power,
God said that Moses would never enter the
Promised Land.

The Bronze Serpent

Shortly after, the people again murmured,
asking why Moses had brought them to a
wilderness, where there was neither food nor
water. God heard their wicked complaints and
sent serpents into their camp, whose bite killed

a great many. Moses prayed that God would have mercy on the people, and the Lord ordered him to make a bronze serpent and set it up on a pole. He did so, and all who looked upon it were healed.

This serpent was a figure of our Savior nailed to the Cross; for as the Israelites who looked upon it were cured, so all who with faith look up to Christ are cured of the wounds of sin. Think of this every time you see a cross.

The Death of Moses

The time had now come for Moses to die; so he called his people together, reminded them of all that God had done for them, ordered them to keep the Commandments, and named Joshua as his successor.

When he had finished speaking, he went up to the top of Mount Nebo, from which the Lord showed him Canaan, the Promised Land. Full of faith and thanks to God for all His favors, Moses died at the age of 120 years.

The Israelites Enter the Promised Land

After the death of Moses, the Lord commanded Joshua to lead the Israelites across the river Jordan into Canaan. On the banks of the river the same miracle that had taken place at the passage of the Red Sea was repeated: the water rolled back, leaving a dry passage.

When the Israelites had crossed over, they encamped near Jericho, where they celebrated the feast of the Pasch. This feast was kept every year in memory of their release from Egypt.

Jericho was a large city, surrounded by strong walls. God commanded the Israelites to march around this city for seven days. On the seventh day they sounded the trumpets of jubilee and carried with them the Ark of the Covenant — a box made of most precious wood, covered inside and out with gold, in which were kept the two tablets of the Law.

At the sound of these trumpets and the shouts of the people, the walls fell in, and the Israelites entered and took the city.

In time Joshua conquered all the country; and thus, after long wandering, the Israelites arrived in the Promised Land.

The Ingratitude of the Israelites

Although Almighty God had been so good to the Israelites, and had given them such a beautiful country, they soon forgot all they owed Him and fell into idolatry. To punish them the Lord for a while allowed their enemies to overcome them and make them slaves.

Samuel

When slavery had taught the Israelites sorrow for their sins, God sent them holy men, called judges. One of them was named Samuel.

His parents were very pious people, who for a long while had had no children. They prayed God to send them a son; and just as He listened to the prayer of Elizabeth, eleven hundred years afterward, so He heard their prayer and gave them Samuel.

When the little boy was three years old, his mother took him to Heli, the high priest, and consecrated him to God.

One night, when Samuel was sleeping in the Temple, the Lord called him. The boy thought it was Heli and ran to him, but the priest said, "I did not call you, my son. Go back and sleep."

The call was repeated three times, so Samuel knew it was the Lord and cried out, "Speak, Lord, for Your servant hears." Then the Lord told him that He was obliged to punish Heli and his two sons: the father because he was too easy with his sons and had not punished them for their wickedness, and the sons because they offended Him by many sins. Some time after, the sons were killed in battle, and when Heli heard the sad news, he fell backward and broke his neck.

Samuel succeeded Heli as judge and ruled wisely and well; but when he grew old, he appointed his sons judges over Israel.

The sons were not like their father: they did not fear God, and the people became dissatisfied and asked for a king.

This did not please Samuel, because he wished that God alone should be King of Israel. But the Lord bade him do as the people wanted; so he anointed, as their king, Saul, a beautiful and brave youth of the tribe of Benjamin.

At first God was with Saul and gave him victory over his enemies; but Saul afterward disobeyed God and was cut off from the throne of Israel.

David

At the command of God, Samuel went to Bethlehem, to the house of Jesse, whose youngest son, David, was chosen by God to replace Saul. David was in the fields, tending his father's flocks, when Samuel arrived.

Samuel sent for him and anointed him.

As the Spirit of the Lord departed from Saul, he became sad; then he ordered his servants to find someone who could play upon the harp and cheer him with its music. One of the servants told him of David, who was a skillful player, so Saul sent for him and was so much pleased with David's playing that he made him his armor-bearer.

David and Goliath

A war broke out between the Israelites and the Philistines, their chief enemy, and as the three oldest sons of Jesse were in the army with Saul, David returned home to his father.

When the two armies were drawn up opposite each other, a terrible giant named Goliath came forth from the Philistine camp and dared any of the Israelites to fight him hand to hand.

Although Saul was a great warrior, he and his entire army were frightened at this, and none of them dared meet Goliath. For forty days the giant repeated his challenge.

At the end of that time, David came to the camp to see his brother. He saw Goliath, heard his words, and was grieved that no one had the courage to fight him. Going to Saul, David said, "I will fight this Philistine."

At first the king would not let him attempt it, but, as David insisted, the king gave him a suit of armor and a helmet of brass.

David was not used to such things, and he could not wear them; but, choosing five smooth stones out of the brook, and taking his sling in his hand, he went forth to meet the giant.

Goliath, seeing this fair young man come out to fight him, thought that he would have an easy victory, but when they came near to each other, David took one of the stones that he carried with him, put it into his sling, and swung it rapidly around and around. The stone flew out and struck the giant on the forehead with such force that he fell to the ground. David ran up, drew the sword of Goliath from its sheath and cut off his head.

When the Philistines saw this, they were frightened and fled, and the Israelites followed and killed many of them.

This victory of David over Goliath was a figure of our Savior's victory over the Devil; for, as David conquered Goliath with a staff and five smooth stones, so did our blessed Lord conquer the Devil by His Cross and His five wounds.

After Saul's death David was chosen king of Israel. He ruled for forty years, and when he died, he left a great kingdom and a great name.

Solomon

David was succeeded by his son Solomon, who at first loved the Lord and walked in his father's footsteps. One night the Lord appeared to him and bade him ask whatever he wanted. Solomon asked for wisdom to rule over his

people with justice. The Lord was so well pleased with this that He gave him not only wisdom, but also riches, honor, and a long life.

One day two women came to the king, asking him to decide a dispute they had. The one said, "I and this woman lived together in the same house, and we each had a baby boy. One night her child died, and while I was asleep, she took my boy and placed her dead child beside me in the bed. In the morning I saw that the child was not mine." The other woman denied this, and there seemed no way to settle the dispute.

Then Solomon ordered the living child to be cut in two, and half to be given to one woman and half to the other. The true mother's heart could not bear that harm should come to her darling boy, and she cried out, "My lord, give her the child, and do not kill him!" But the other woman said, "Let him be divided."

Then Solomon, pointing to the true mother, answered, "Give the child to this woman, for she is his mother." And the people were astonished at the wisdom of the king.

Solomon built a temple to Almighty God at Jerusalem. It was the grandest and most beautiful the world has ever seen. For twenty years Solomon did all that he could do for the glory of God, but when he grew old, he fell into sin and oppressed his people until they became discontented and rebellious.

The Division of the Kingdom

At Solomon's death the Jewish people divided into two kingdoms, Israel and Judah. Jerusalem remained the capital of Judah, while Samaria became the capital of Israel.

The people of Israel soon fell into idolatry, and although God did much to save them, both by humbling and by cheering them, they were so self-willed and stubborn that they would not obey His laws.

At last, to punish them for their sins, He allowed the Assyrians, a pagan nation, to conquer them and make them slaves, and in a short time there was nothing left of them as a nation.

The people of Judah, too, gave themselves up for a while to idolatry and sin. To punish them, God allowed the Babylonians to burn the Temple of Solomon, to destroy Jerusalem, and later on to carry the entire people of Judah to Babylon, where they were kept as prisoners for seventy years. At the end of that time, when they were truly sorry for their sins, God led the Jews back to their own country.

They at once rebuilt Jerusalem and the Temple, and for two hundred years they lived peacefully and happily.

About 323 years before the birth of our Savior, the Jews fought not only with other nations but among themselves, until at last the Romans, then the greatest nation on the earth, were called upon to settle their disputes. Soon the Romans with their armies filled the country, seized the government, and made Herod king of the Jews. Thus ended the kingdom of Judah.

The time had now come for our Lord Jesus Christ to be born into the world to save man from sin, and open the gates of heaven, which had been closed by the fall of our first parents.

The Story
of the
New Testament

An Angel Visits Zachary

Long, long ago there lived two holy women named Elizabeth and Mary, who were cousins. Elizabeth was an old woman, and as she had no little children, she and her husband, who was named Zachary, used to pray to God to give them a child. One day, when Zachary was at God's altar in the Temple of the Lord, the angel Gabriel came to him and said, "God has heard your prayer. He will send you a child, whom you must call John. He will do much good to his people and teach them about the Christ to come. He must never taste wine, because God will make him strong."

Zachary was frightened when he heard all this and said to the angel, "I am an old man

and my wife is old," and he doubted what God had said to him by the angel.

Zachary Is Punished

Now God was angry with Zachary for doubting that He could send him a child, but not very angry, because Zachary was a good man; so God told the angel to tell Zachary that He was displeased with him and would make him dumb until the baby John was born.

So then and there in the Temple Zachary was made dumb.

When he came out, he could not speak to his friends, but made signs to them, so they knew that he was dumb, and they said, "Something has happened.He has seen some sight — a vision."

The Annunciation

After six months had passed, God sent this same angel Gabriel to a town called Nazareth, where the Virgin Mary lived.

And so the angel went to Mary's house, and when he came into the room, he said to Mary, "Hail, full of grace, the Lord is with you!"

And Mary felt troubled, for she thought, "This is a strange way of speaking to me."

Then the angel said to her, "Fear not, Mary, for you have found favor with God. And behold you will conceive in your womb and bear a Son; and you shall call His name Jesus. He will be great and will be called the Son of the Most High."

And Mary said, "How can this be?"

And the angel said, "The power of God will do it." He told her of her cousin Elizabeth, who, old as she was, would have a son in three months.

Then Mary said, "Behold the handmaid of the Lord; be it done to me according to your word." And the angel went away.

Mary Visits Elizabeth

Mary was glad to hear about Elizabeth, and she went in haste to pay her a visit.

Elizabeth was very glad to see her cousin and thus saluted Mary, "Blessed are you among women, and blessed is the fruit of your womb. And why has God done this to me, that the mother of my Lord should come to me? You are blessed, Mary, because you believed; therefore God will do to you what He has said."

Mary then sang a beautiful song, the words of which God put into her heart, "My soul magnifies the Lord, and my spirit rejoices in God my Savior, because He has regarded the humility of His handmaid. For behold, from

henceforth all generations will call me blessed,
because He who is mighty has done great
things to me, and holy is His name."

This is a part of the song which is called
the *Magnificat*.

Mary stayed with Elizabeth for three
months, and then she returned home.

John Is Born

After a time Elizabeth's little boy was born, and all her friends came to see her and wish her joy. When the baby was eight days old, they had a ceremony called the circumcision, and they said, "You must call him after his father's name." But Elizabeth said, "No, call him John."

And they were surprised, because none in her family were ever called by that name. As Zachary was dumb, they made signs to him to know what name they should call the boy, and he showed them that he wanted something to write on. So they brought him a writing tablet, and he wrote on it only these words: "John *is* his name." And they were again surprised.

As soon as Zachary had written this, God rewarded him for his obedience, and his tongue was loosed and he spoke, blessing God. The neighbors wondered and told everyone all about what great and strange things had been done.

And Zachary was told by God many things his son John would do when he grew up.

The Birth of Jesus

At this time there was a great king in Rome named Caesar, and he wanted to know how many people there were in the world; so he gave orders that everyone should go to the town in which he was born to have his name written on a list.

Joseph and Mary were living at Nazareth; but as that was not the town of Joseph's birth, he told Mary to get ready and come with him to the town of Bethlehem, because he was of the house and family of David.

They went from Nazareth to Bethlehem; but when they got there, every inn and every house in the town was full of people, and they had no place to sleep.

You may be sure Mary was tired; so Joseph, after looking about, found only a stable, to which he brought Mary. Here Mary's little Son, our Lord and Savior Jesus Christ, was born.

Mary was the best of mothers, and she did all she could for her Child. She wrapped Him up and put Him in the manger — probably because there was straw there, and it was warmer than any other place.

The men who take care of sheep are called shepherds, and some of these men were minding their sheep that night when Jesus was born. All at once a lovely angel came to them when they were out in the fields, and all around the angel was a bright light from God — so bright that the shepherds were afraid.

The angel said to them, "Fear not. I bring you good news of a great joy that will come to all the people, for to you is born this day in the city of David a Savior, who is Christ the Lord. And this will be a sign for you: you will find a Baby wrapped in swaddling clothes and lying in a manger."

When the angel had said this, a great number of angels came and stood with him, and they praised God and in lovely voices sang a song, "Glory to God in the highest; and on earth peace to men of goodwill." After the song, the angels opened their wings and flew up into heaven. It must have been a grand, glad sight for these poor men to see!

The Shepherds thought so and said to one another, "Let us go over to Bethlehem, and let us see this wonder that is come to pass, which the Lord has told us of by His angel."

They left their sheep and went off in great haste to Bethlehem, and they there found Joseph and Mary and the Baby lying in the manger. They knew then that the Child was the Savior and that what the angel had said was true; so they told everyone what they had seen and heard.

Mary kept all these things in her heart and did not forget them. Then the shepherds went back to mind their sheep, and on their way they praised God.

The Three Wise Men

At this time there were three Wise Men who lived in the East, and they went to Jerusalem, to the king, whose name was Herod, and they said to him, "Where is He who is born King of the Jews? We have seen His star, and we have come to adore Him."

Herod did not like to hear of any other king but himself. So he sent word to all the learned men in Jerusalem to come to him, and he said to them, "Where would Christ be born?" And they answered, "In Bethlehem," because it was known long before that that was the town where Christ was to be born.

Herod said to the three Wise Men in secret, "Go to Bethlehem and find out where

the Child is, so that I also may go and adore
Him." They went, and found Jesus with Joseph
and Mary, and they offered Jesus presents of
gold and incense. The three Wise Men were
tired, and they went to rest. In their sleep they
had a dream in which God told them not to go
back to Herod, so they did not.

The Prophecy of Simeon

When the Child was eight days old, Mary and Joseph had that ceremony I told you of before, and the Baby was circumcised and called Jesus.

After forty days Joseph and Mary took Jesus to the city of Jerusalem, where the great Temple was, "to present Him to the Lord," and to offer a sacrifice, according to the law of the Lord, "a pair of turtledoves or two young pigeons."

Now, in Jerusalem there lived a very holy old man whose name was Simeon, and he used to pray to God that he might not die until his eyes had seen the Savior.

So when Joseph and Mary brought the Child Jesus into the Temple, a thought from God came into Simeon's mind, and he said to himself, "I will go to the Temple today."

He went, and there he saw a man and a woman with a Child, and he went up to them and took the lovely Baby from Mary into his own arms. He knew he was right, and he said, "Now, Lord, I am ready to die because You have let me see the Savior with my eyes."

Mary and Joseph were surprised at all this, and Simeon saw surprise in their faces; so he blessed them, and he said to Mary, "This Child is set for the fall and the saving of many" — that is, many will believe in Him and so go to heaven, and many will not believe and so go to hell.

Then he told Mary that she would have great sorrows — so great that they would pierce her soul like a sword.

The Flight into Egypt

When Joseph went to sleep one night, an angel came to him and said, "Get up, and take Mary and the Child into Egypt, and stay there until I tell you to return, for Herod has it in his mind to kill Jesus." Joseph called Mary and told her, and they set out at once for Egypt.

When Herod found out that the Wise Men did not return, he was furious, because he knew they had seen the Child and would not tell him. He was a cruel, wicked man, and he told his soldiers to kill all the baby boys under two years old they could find.

Herod hoped that the soldiers might find Jesus among them and so kill Him! But they did not; and after Herod died, Joseph returned with Jesus and Mary to Nazareth.

The Feast of the Passover

In those days there was a great feast in the Temple at Jerusalem every year, and people from all parts of the country used to go to Jerusalem for this feast.

Jesus was a lovely boy, and was growing strong and tall and more lovely every year. When He was twelve years old, Joseph and Mary took Him to Jerusalem for one of these feasts, and many of their friends and relations went too, and they all stayed there some days.

On their way home again they missed Jesus. Mary thought He was with Joseph, and Joseph thought He was with Mary. When they found it was not so, they said, "Oh, He is with our relatives." But when they asked their friends, they said, "No, we have not seen Him."

So Mary and Joseph went back to Jerusalem
and looked for Him for three days. At last they
went to the Temple, where they found Jesus
sitting with a number of priests and learned
people, and He was asking them questions and
answering theirs in a wise and clever way — so
wise that all these learned men were surprised.

When Mary saw Him, she said to Him, "Son, why have You treated us this way? Your father and I have been looking for You anxiously."

Then Jesus said to them, "How is it that you sought me? Did you not know that I must be in my Father's house?" Mary and Joseph could not tell why He had said this to them, but Mary kept all these words in her heart to think about them.

Then Jesus went back with them to Nazareth and obeyed them in all things.

The Baptism of Jesus

Many years passed, and John, the son of Zachary, who had been living in a lonely place — the desert — praying to God, was told by God that now he should tell the people what to do. So he left the desert and came to the river Jordan, the same river that had rolled back for the Jews hundreds of years before.

Here John called all the people around him and told them of God — that they should never more be wicked.

After he had baptized them, he told them
such holy things that at last the people said
that he must be the Christ.

But John was pained at this, and told them
he was not worthy to tie the shoes of Christ —
which meant that even as a servant, he was not
worthy to serve Jesus Christ.

One day Jesus also came to the river Jordan to be baptized by John. When John saw Jesus coming, he said, "Behold the Lamb of God; behold Him who takes away the sins of the world."

After the baptism a wonderful thing took place. The sky opened, and the Holy Spirit, in the shape of a dove, flew down to Jesus, and the people heard a voice from heaven saying, "This is my beloved Son, in whom I am well pleased."

Jesus at this time was thirty years old.

The Marriage Feast

Jesus loved His mother, Mary, very much, and He did what she asked Him to do. There was one day a wedding at a place called Cana, and Jesus and Mary were invited to it.

At the feast all the wine was used, for there was not enough, and when Mary saw this, she told Jesus that there was no wine.

Jesus did not want to use His power yet; but He could not deny His Mother, as we shall see.

He said to Mary, "What is it to us if they
have no wine?" But Mary knew in her heart
that Jesus would do what she wanted. So she
said to the servants who were waiting at the
table, "Do whatever He tells you to do."

Now, in the room there were six large
stone jars, with a little water in them, and

Jesus, calling to Him the servants, said to them, "Fill the water-pots with water." And they filled them up to the brim.

Then Jesus said, "Draw the water out now, and take it to the butler," and they did. But the man did not know, when he had tasted it, where the wine had come from, for Jesus had changed the water into wine. The guests at the table said, "Our host has kept the best wine for the last!"

This is the beginning of the miracles Jesus did that manifested His glory; and His disciples believed in Him.

Jesus then went to His own city, Nazareth.

The Draught of Fishes

Such crowds of people would now follow Jesus to hear Him speak of God that one day, when He was standing near the shore of a lake, they pressed so close to Him that He had to get away.

He called two fishermen who were washing their nets, and He said to one of them, whose name was Simon Peter, "Draw the boat back a little from the land." Then, sitting in the boat, Jesus talked to the people on shore and taught them many things.

When He had finished speaking, Jesus did a very kind thing for the fisherman. He told the man to row out into the deep water and let out his nets to catch fish. But Simon Peter said to Him, "We have worked all night, Master, and have caught none; but still, as You tell me, I will let down my net."

And he did so; and the net was so full at once of fishes that it was not large enough to hold them.

So Simon Peter called out to James and John, his partners, to come and help him; and they filled their boats so full with the fishes that the boats were almost sinking.

Peter was surprised at this, and so were the others; and when they had brought their ships to land, they left them and stayed with Jesus.

Jesus always chose poor men as His companions, and He gave them great honor.

In this way, at different times He called unto Him His disciples to help Him to teach and preach, and they were called Apostles of Jesus.

There were twelve of them, and their names were Peter, Andrew, James, John, Philip, Bartholomew, Matthew, Thomas, James, Simon, Jude, and Judas.

The Sermon on the Mount

Jesus was always doing good to the people, curing them when sick; and He had a kind way of telling them stories, to make them know what He meant.

One day Jesus went up a high mountain and He brought His disciples with Him, and a great number of people; and He gave them a sermon, and with His own lips taught them how to pray.

He told them to "pray always" and then taught them that prayer you say so often — the Our Father.

The Man Cured of Paralysis

After that sermon on the hill, Jesus told the people that He had the power to forgive sin; and to show that He had this power He worked this miracle:

He was one day preaching to the learned men in a house in the town of Capharnaum, and the house was so full of people that no one could get in at the door.

There was a poor sick man in the town who was paralyzed and could not walk, so he asked four of his friends to carry him on his bed to the house where Jesus was.

In the East the roofs are flat and have a hole in them, so that people can go on the roof for air. The crowd being great, they could not carry the sick man in by the door, but they carried him up on the roof and let him down on his bed through the hole to Jesus.

Jesus was so pleased at their faith, and at their trying so hard to see Him, that when He saw the sick man, He said, "Son, your sins are forgiven. Arise, take up your bed, and walk."

At once the man got up quite cured, and thanked Jesus, praising God. At this the people wondered and said, "We never saw anything like this."

The Pool of Bethzatha

After a time Jesus went to Jerusalem.

Now, at Jerusalem there was a pond of water called the Well of Bethzatha. At certain times, God used to send an angel to this pond to stir it up.

Many people, the sick and the lame and the blind, used to stay near this pond to watch for the angel; for when the angel visited the pond, the person who got first into the water would be cured.

There was one poor man who had been waiting at this pond for thirty-eight years, but

he was so sick that when he would try to get
into the water after the angel had come, some
other man, stronger than he was, would get in
first and so be cured.

Jesus heard of this sick man and went to
him, and said to him, "Do you want to be
healed?"

And the sick man said, "Sir, I have no man to put me into the pool when the water is stirred. While I am going, another steps down before me."

Jesus said to him, "Rise, take up your pallet, and walk." And at once the lame man was made well, and he took up his pallet and walked.

The Storm at Sea in Galilee

One day Jesus said to His disciples, "Let us go over to the other side of the lake." They had been teaching the people near a lake called Genesareth, and He got into a little ship with His disciples.

After they had been out on the water a short time, Jesus, who was tired, went to sleep. While He was asleep, a storm of wind came on, and the boat began to fill with water, and they were in danger.

The disciples, being afraid, went to Jesus and awoke Him and said, "Master, we are sinking." So Jesus, getting up, told the wind and the sea to be quiet, and it became quite calm.

The Daughter of Jairus

When the ship had crossed the lake and come to the shore, a man named Jairus came to Jesus and went down on his knees before Him, saying, "My only little girl, just twelve years old, is dying," and Jesus went with the man to his house.

But such a crowd pressed around Jesus that they could not move easily. A sick woman touched the robe of Jesus and was instantly cured.

Just as they got near the house of Jairus, a servant came out and said to Jairus, "Do not trouble Jesus, for your daughter is dead."

Hearing the servant say this, Jesus said to the girl's father, "Fear not. Only believe, and she shall be safe."

When they went into the house — the father and mother and Jesus and a few others — they saw the little girl lying dead, and they were all in great sorrow, and they wept bitterly.

But Jesus said, "Do not weep. The maid is not dead, but sleeping." And the people

laughed at Jesus in scorn, because they knew
she was dead. But Jesus, taking her by the
hand, cried out, saying, "Maid, arise."

At once she came to life and got up, and
Jesus told them to give her something to eat.
The parents were very happy and surprised at
this wonder that our Lord did for them.

The Loaves and Fishes

Once a great crowd — five thousand people — followed Jesus to a lonely place, far from a town, to hear Him preach. It was evening, and no one had anything to eat. So the disciples said to Jesus, "Send away the people, so that they may go to the towns and buy food."

But Jesus said to them, "You give them something to eat."

And they said, "We have no more than five loaves and two fishes, unless we go and buy food for all these people."

Jesus said, "Make them sit down by fifties in a company." And they did so and made them all sit down.

And Jesus took the five loaves and the two fishes, and He looked up to heaven and blessed them; and He broke the bread and gave it to His disciples to give to the people.

And all these five thousand people had so much to eat from the five loaves and the two fishes that, when they had had enough, twelve baskets were filled with the broken pieces. This was a great wonder, and it was done to show us what Jesus does on our altars.

Jesus Walks on the Sea

After this wonder, Jesus told His disciples to go in a boat across the lake and wait for Him. Jesus liked to pray alone, so He sent away all the people and the disciples. The disciples waited for Jesus in the boat, and a storm came on with the night.

Now, Jesus saw the boat out on the lake, and He knew His disciples were afraid, so He walked out on the sea. He did not swim, but walked on the water, just as we walk on land.

When the disciples saw Jesus coming to them in this strange way, they were afraid, and they said to one another, "It is a ghost."

But Jesus spoke to them, saying, "Be of good heart. It is I. Fear not."

And Peter, who was in the boat, said, "Lord, if it be You, bid me come to You upon the waters," and Jesus said, "Come." Peter, who saw how rough the sea was, and how the wind blew, was afraid, but he stepped out of the boat, and when he began to sink, he cried out, saying, "Lord, save me." And at once Jesus put out His hand and took hold of Peter's, saying, "O you of little faith, why did you doubt?"

They walked together to the boat, and the wind ceased. The disciples, when they had seen this, adored Jesus and said, "Indeed You are the Son of God."

The Transfiguration

Jesus had now taught His disciples many things and told them of many things that would happen to Him, and He had made Peter the chief of His Apostles.

One day Jesus took Peter, James, and John with Him to a high mountain, and while He was there, His face shone as the sun, and His clothes became white as snow, and two good men, Moses and Elijah, who had lived long ago, were seen talking to Him.

When the disciples saw this great sight, they fell flat on their faces, and they heard a voice from heaven say, "This is my beloved Son, in whom I am well pleased. Listen to Him." Jesus saw how afraid His disciples were, and He went to them and touched them, saying, "Arise, and fear not." And, lifting up their eyes, they saw no one, only Jesus.

After this Jesus told them that one of them would betray Him to His enemies and that He would be put to death, but that after three days He would rise again.

Jesus, the Children's Friend

One day the disciples were talking to Jesus about heaven, and they wanted to know who would be the greatest in heaven.

There was a little child passing by at the time, and Jesus called the child to Him and said to His disciples, "Amen, I say to you, unless you be converted [made good] and become as little children, you shall not enter into the kingdom of heaven."

Jesus then told them what a bad thing it was to teach sin to little children, or to one another. He said that it would have been better that those who teach sin to His little ones had never been born, or that a stone had been tied around their necks and they were drowned in the sea.

You see, Jesus loved little children who were good, and grown-up people must be good too, and as simple as little children. You must never tell anything wrong to another, or teach sin to those younger than you, because you know now what Jesus says.

Jesus at this time also told fathers and mothers and husbands and wives how they should live.

There were many mothers in the crowd, and they had their little children with them. When Jesus had finished speaking, the mothers brought their little children to Jesus so that He might lay His hands upon them and bless them; but the disciples thought it was too much trouble to Jesus, so they told the mothers not to bring the children.

But Jesus was not pleased with this, for He loved little children, and He said, "Let the little children come to me, and do not stop them, for the kingdom of heaven is for such."

And then Jesus blessed each little child. Little children ought to love Jesus very much for this.

The Blind Man

When Jesus and His Apostles had come to a town called Jericho with a number of people, a blind man, who heard that Jesus was passing, called out to Him, saying, "Jesus, Son of David, have mercy on me!"

And Jesus stood still and told the people to bring the blind man to Him. So they brought the blind man, and Jesus said to him, "What do you want me to do for you?"

And the blind man said, "Master, let me receive my sight." Then Jesus said to him,

"Go your way. Your faith has made you whole," and at once he saw, and he followed Jesus with the other people.

At times the people and the Apostles could not understand Jesus. To help them understand, He would often explain what He meant by telling them stories.

The Good Samaritan

Once when Jesus was teaching, a man who was a lawyer thought he would test Jesus, so he said to Him, "Master, what must I do to possess eternal life?"

And Jesus said, "What is written in the law? How do you read it?"

And the lawyer said, "It is written: You shall love the Lord Your God with your whole heart, and with your whole soul, and with all your strength, and with all your mind; and your neighbor as yourself."

And Jesus said, "You have answered right. Do this and you shall live."

And the man said, "Who is my neighbor?"

Jesus then told him his story: "Once there was a man who was going on a journey from Jerusalem to Jericho, and on his way some robbers met him. They tore off all his clothes, took his money, struck him and hurt him, and left him like a dead man by the side of the road.

"After a time, a priest went down the same way and, seeing him, passed by.

"In like manner, a Levite, when he was near the place and saw him, passed by.

"But at last a Samaritan, being on a journey, came near him and, seeing him, was moved with pity, and going up to him, bound up his wounds, pouring in oil and wine, and putting the man on his own mule, brought him to an inn and took care of him.

"The next day he had to go away, but he left money with the owner of the inn, and told him to take care of the man, and that if the money was not enough, he would give him more on his return."

Then Jesus said to the lawyer, "Which of these three, in your opinion, was neighbor to him who fell among the robbers?"

And he answered, "He who showed mercy to him."

Then Jesus said to him, "Go and do in like manner."

In this story Jesus teaches us who is our neighbor and that we should do to others what we would like them to do to us. If you were hurt or sick, you would like someone to

be kind to you; you should, then, be always
kind to others — to the ugly, the dirty, and the
cross, as well as to nice people, because they are
your neighbors.

A neighbor in this sense does not mean only
the person who lives next door, but every man,
woman, and child.

To Be Forgiven, We Must Forgive

One day Peter asked Jesus how often he should forgive his friends if they annoyed or hurt him. Would it be often enough if he forgave them seven times?

But Jesus told him no, that even if Peter were to forgive them, not seven times, but seventy-seven times, it would not be enough.

And then Jesus told him a story: "Once there was a king who had a servant who owed him ten thousand talents, and the man had no way of paying this money.

"The king sent for him and said, 'Pay me the money you owe me,' but the man said, 'I cannot.'

"Then the king ordered that all this man had and loved in the world should be sold in order that he should be paid.

"But the man fell on his knees and begged the king to wait and to have patience with him. The king had pity on him, and said, 'Well, never mind. I forgive you, and I will not ask you to pay me the money at all.' So the man thanked him and went away.

"Just as he went out of the house, he met a fellow servant of his who owed him one hundred pence, and he caught hold of him by the throat and said to him in a rough way, 'Pay me what you owe me!'

"His friend said, 'Wait a little, and I will pay you.' But he would not wait, and he took him and put him in prison until he paid the debt.

"Some people who knew how kind the king had been to this man went and told the king how cruel he had been to his friend. The king, hearing it, was very angry and sent for him.

"When he had come, the king said to him, 'You wicked man! I forgave you all your debt because you asked it, and you would not show the same mercy to your friend.' So he was sent off to prison until he had paid all his debt."

Jesus told Peter this story to explain to him that we must forgive others if we wish the King (God) to forgive us.

God forgives us very, very often, and yet we sometimes find it very hard to make up with our friends, and to forgive and forget from our hearts when we have had a little dispute.

The Lost Sheep

Once when Jesus was teaching, a number of men who were sinners came to hear Him, and there were present also some men who thought themselves very good.

These men complained because Jesus spoke to and ate with sinners; so Jesus told these men some stories: "Once there was a man who owned sheep. He had a hundred sheep in a fold, and one day a little lamb got out of the fold and was lost.

"The shepherd left all the other sheep and went to look for this lamb. At last he found it, and the poor little lamb was tired; so he took it on his shoulders and carried it back to the fold.

"Then the shepherd, going home, told his friends he had found the lost lamb, and he said to them, 'Rejoice with me, because I have found my sheep that was lost.' "

Jesus told them what this story meant: heaven was like the sheepfold; the sheep were the people, and the lost lamb was a wicked person — one who had once been good, but had become bad; the shepherd was God, who loved this wicked little lost lamb and went after it to find it, leaving the good sheep behind.

And Jesus further said that there was more joy in heaven over one sinner becoming good and doing penance than over ninety-nine good people who do not need penance.

The Prodigal Son

Jesus also told this story: "Once a man had two sons. He was a rich man, had a grand house, and lived in great state. But the younger son thought the house and life were too quiet; he wanted to go out into the world and enjoy himself, and have a good time.

"One day he came to his father and said, 'I know you are going to divide some money between my elder brother and me; give me my share now, and let me go away.'

"The father was pained at this; still he did not refuse his son, but gave him his share of money. After a few days, this younger son said goodbye to his father and his brother, and took with him some bad companions, and left his father's house. He went away to a country a long way off, and there led a very bad, wicked life.

"In a short time he had spent all his money, and, you may be quite sure, his friends then left him, because he could treat them no more.

"What could he do then? He was in a strange country, and he had no money.

"At last he was truly miserable — he was hungry and had no clothes.

"One day he went to a man and asked him for work, but he looked so poor and dirty that the man said, 'I can give you no work in my house, but you may go to my farm and mind the pigs.'

"So he went and minded the pigs, but he got no food except what the pigs did not like.

"This he found so hard, and he was so miserable, that he began to think of home and of the servants that his father had; and he said to himself, 'How many servants in my father's house eat bread, and I am here dying of hunger!' So he said, 'I will arise and will go to my father, and say to him, "Father, I have sinned against heaven and before you. I am not worthy to be called your son. Make me as one of your hired servants." '

"He started at once on his journey to his father.

"The father loved his son and used to look out every evening for him, hoping he would come back. One evening he was looking out as usual, and he saw, a great way off, his son, and he went to meet him and, running up to him, put his arms around his neck and kissed him.

"But the son fell on his knees and said to him, 'Father, I have sinned against heaven and before you. I am not now worthy to be called your son.'

"But the father was so glad to see him that he kissed him again and again, and put fine clothes on him, and told his servants to make a great feast, because his son, who was lost and was as one dead, was found again. Then they had a great feast, and music and dancing.

"The elder son, who was working in a field, heard the music and came to the house to see what it was for, asking one of the servants he met what it all meant. And the servant told him, 'Your brother has returned, and your father has made a great feast because he has come back safe.'

"At this the elder brother was very angry, and he would not go into the house. His father, hearing it, came out to him, and tried to coax him in; but he would not come and said to his

father, 'I have done all you asked me to do for so many years, and have been good, and have not spent your money, but you never made a feast for me as you have for my brother, who spent all his money and led a bad life.'

"But the father said to him, 'Son, you are always with me, and all I have is yours; but it was fitting that we should make merry and be glad, for your brother was dead and is come to life again; he was lost and is found.' "

This story, too, was told to teach us that God will forgive sinners; but we must be sorry, as the younger son was, and confess our sins to a priest, as he did to his father. And as he was willing to be a servant in his father's house because of his sins, so we must be humble and willing to suffer for our sins. The good son, you see, was doubly rewarded, for the father said, "Son, all I have is yours" — not only his own share, but his father's also.

The Rich Man and Lazarus

Jesus told this story to His disciples: "There once lived a very rich man, and he had a fine house and grounds. To the gates of this house a poor man, whose name was Lazarus, would crawl daily. He was hungry and covered with sores. He lay there at the gate in hopes the rich man would send him some crumbs to eat.

"But the rich man did not. He was dressed in grand clothes, and had rich food to eat, and plenty of wine to drink; but he never sent even a crumb to the poor man he knew to be at his gate.

"This poor man was very ill, and his sores were so bad that dogs used to come and lick them. At length Lazarus died, and the angels came and carried him to the place of rest where Abraham is. The rich man died also, 'but he was buried in hell.'

"When he was in hell and burning in pain and torment, he lifted his eyes and saw this poor man with Abraham. The rich man cried out, 'Father Abraham, have mercy on me, and send Lazarus so that he may dip the tip of his finger in water to cool my tongue, for I am burned in this flame.'

"But Abraham said, 'Son, you received good things in the world — food and wine and riches and health — but Lazarus did not have all these good things. He now has his reward and has comfort, and you have your reward in misery.' Abraham told him besides that none could go from heaven to hell, or from hell to heaven."

Jesus had told His disciples many things, but there was yet a great deal for them to know. He had made Peter head of His disciples, because Peter had the most faith and had said that Jesus was "the Son of the living God."

He also told them that soon He would be put to a cruel death and that one of His disciples would give Him up into the hands of His enemies.

Christ Raises Lazarus to Life

In a village called Bethany lived another Lazarus, with his two sisters, Martha and Mary. Jesus loved this family very much and often went to visit them.

One day Martha and Mary sent word to Jesus that Lazarus His friend was very ill. When the messenger told our Lord, Jesus said, "Lazarus is sick so that the glory of God and my power may be shown in him."

Jesus was staying in the country then; and two days after He had been told that Lazarus was so ill, He called His disciples and said to them, "Lazarus, our friend, is asleep, and we must go to Bethany and wake him up." But His disciples said, "Lord, if he is sleeping, he will be well."

But Jesus meant that Lazarus was dead. So He said to them plainly, "Lazarus is dead, and I am glad for your sakes that I was not there, that you may believe. But let us go to him."

When they arrived at Bethany, Lazarus had been dead four days, and in his grave. In those countries people are buried the day they die.

Martha, when she heard Jesus had come, went to see Him, and said to Him, "Lord, if You had been here, my brother would not have died; but I know that whatever You ask of God, He will give it to You."

Jesus asked where Mary was, and Martha said, "She is in the house with our friends and many others, who came to mourn with us. I will go tell her You asked for her."

When Mary heard that Jesus had asked for her, she rose with haste, left her friends, and went to Jesus. Falling down at His feet, she said, "Lord, if You had been here, my brother would not have not died."

Jesus, when He saw her tears, and the others who had followed her weeping also, was very, very sorry for her, and He was full of trouble.

He asked, "Where have you buried him?" And they said to Him, "Lord, come and see." And Jesus wept. Therefore they said, "Behold, how He loved him!"

But some of them said, "If He opened the eyes of the man born blind, could He not have kept this man from dying?"

Jesus, when He came to the grave, over which there was a stone placed, directed them, "Take away the stone." Martha, when she heard this, did not want to have it moved, and said to Jesus, "Lord, by this time there will be a smell, for he is now buried four days."

But Jesus told her to have faith and she would see the power of God. So the stone was rolled away.

Jesus then gave thanks to God and cried out with a loud voice, "Lazarus, come forth!" At once, just as he was, all wrapped in cloths, out came Lazarus from his grave, and Jesus told them to untie the cloths.

What joy it must have been to Martha and
Mary, and how glad Jesus must have felt to see
the joy of these friends, for Jesus likes to make
people happy. All those who had seen this great
wonder went about the country and even to
Jerusalem, telling how Lazarus, who was four
days dead, was brought to life again by Jesus.

When wicked people who had power in Jerusalem heard of it, they were jealous of Jesus and hated Him. They made up their minds that the first chance they had, they would kill Him.

Jesus Rides into Jerusalem

About a week after Lazarus had come to life again, Jesus had supper with Lazarus and Mary and Martha, and the next day He said to His disciples, "It is time we went to Jerusalem."

When they had come to Mount Olivet, Jesus told two of His disciples to go to the next village, and that they would there find tied to a gate an ass with its young one, called a colt. No man had ridden yet on this colt.

Jesus told them, "When you find this colt, the man you see minding it will ask you what you want, and you are to say you want the colt, for the Lord has need of it, and then he will let you take it."

And the disciples did as Jesus had instructed them. When they brought the colt to Jesus, it

had no harness or saddle on it, so they spread
their clothes over its back and Jesus sat
on it.

A very great crowd of people came, and
they cut down boughs of trees, carried palm-
branches in their hands, and strewed their
clothes and boughs along the way for Jesus to

ride over. They shouted and sang, "Blessed is He who comes in the name of the Lord!" and so they entered Jerusalem in great joy.

The whole city came out to meet them, and they said, "Who is this?" and the people said, "This is Jesus."

Jesus went to the Temple, and crowds came with Him, and they brought to Him the blind, the deaf, the lame, the dumb, and all sick persons, and Jesus cured them, so that they were all glad and filled with joy. Even the little children called out, "Hosanna to the Son of David! Blessed be the Son of David!"

The high priests and learned men, hearing the children, were angry, and they asked Jesus if He heard what the children said. Jesus always loved little children and must have liked their song best of all, for He said, "Yes, I hear. 'Out of the mouths of infants and of sucklings You have perfected praise.' "

The Widow's Mite

When Jesus was in the Temple, He saw a poor widow drop a penny into the money-box.

He was so pleased that He called His disciples to Him and told them that this poor woman had given more than all the rich, and her reward would be greater, because she gave all she had, and the rich gave only what they did not want.

The Paschal Lamb

You remember that the Jews had some laws given them by God, which they observed carefully. One was how to celebrate the great feast of Passover, when they killed a lamb and ate a special kind of bread.

When the time came, Jesus told Peter and John to go to the city and prepare a room for this feast. Jesus told them that in the city they would meet a man carrying a jug of water on his head, and that they should follow this man into any house he entered. They were to ask the owner of that house where was the room for Jesus and His disciples to eat the lamb, and he would show them a furnished room, all ready.

In the evening, Jesus came to this place with His twelve disciples and ate what is called the Lord's Last Supper.

The Washing of the Feet

After supper was over, Jesus got up from the table, and tied a towel around Himself, and taking a basin of water, washed the feet of His disciples and dried them with the towel.

When Jesus came to Peter to wash his feet, Peter did not want to let our Lord do such a humble act, and said, "Lord, will You wash my feet?" And Jesus said, "Yes."

But Peter said to Him, "You shall never wash my feet." And Jesus answered him, "If I do not wash you, you shall have no part with me." Rather than that this should be the case, Peter said, "Lord, wash not only my feet, but also my hands and my head."

Jesus then told His disciples why He had washed their feet. He said, "You call me Master and Lord, and you say well, for so I am. If, then, I, being Your Lord and Master, have washed your feet, you should also wash one another's feet. For I have given you an example, that as I have done to you, so you do also."

This was to teach His disciples, and us also, to be humble and clean (good) of heart. Jesus knew even while He was speaking that one of His disciples there was not clean (good) of heart, and his name was Judas.

The Blessed Sacrament

After Jesus had washed His disciples' feet, and while they were eating, He said, "Amen, I say to you, one of you is about to betray me."

The disciples were sorry to hear this, and each said, "Is it I, Lord?" And Judas, who did betray Him, said, "Is it I, Master?" Jesus said to him, "You have said it."

And while they were at supper, Jesus took bread, blessed and broke it, and gave it to His disciples and said, "Take and eat; this is my body." And taking the chalice, He gave thanks, and gave drink to them, saying, "Drink of it, all of you; for this is my blood."

My dear children, this was the greatest, kindest, and most loving act that even God could do. Jesus could do no more than this. Never forget these words of Jesus: "This is my body," and "This is my blood." Jesus, then, at this feast, changed the bread into His body and the wine into His blood. No one can understand this, but when you are older, you will know a little better.

When you go to church and bend your knee at the altar, you do so because you are told the Blessed Sacrament is there. You know now how it came there. The Blessed Sacrament is Jesus. Jesus gave us Himself at that Last Supper; and although we cannot see Him as He was then, as a man speaking to His disciples, yet the Blessed Sacrament is Jesus, and He is there on our altar, hidden in that Host, the very same good, kind, loving Jesus who spoke to His disciples at the Last Supper.

We should often go to our churches to see Jesus and talk to Him, to ask Him for everything we want. No little thing is too small and no big thing is too great to ask Jesus for, and you know He loves little children.

Jesus Speaks of His Passion

The sad time had now come when Jesus was to be so cruelly put to death, and for us. We must never forget that it was for each of us that Jesus died.

Some days before, Judas, the bad disciple, had gone to the high priests and offered to betray Jesus to them. For this they agreed to give him thirty pieces of silver.

While our Lord and His disciples were at the Last Supper, Judas left the room to carry out his wicked bargain. Jesus now was sad because He knew that the time had come for Him to suffer.

Jesus told this to His disciples, and He said that soon He must leave them. Peter said that he would never leave Jesus, but would die first.

Jesus then said to him, "Before this very day is over, and before the rooster crows, you will deny me three times — you will deny that you know me."

Jesus in the Garden

Jesus now went to garden called Gethsemane with His disciples. He was very sad, and He told them not to follow Him, but to stay where they were for a little, as He wished to pray alone.

Jesus then went by Himself and prayed, saying, "My Father, if it be possible, let this chalice pass from me. Nevertheless, not as I will, but as You will."

Jesus then went back to His disciples, but He found them all asleep, and He said to Peter, "What! Could you not watch one hour with me? Watch and pray, that you enter not into temptation; the spirit, indeed, is willing, but the flesh is weak."

Three times Jesus went and prayed and used the same words, and each time He returned to find the disciples fast asleep. Jesus was in such sorrow and trouble in these prayers that He was bathed in agony with sweat, which became as drops of blood trickling to the ground.

He saw all the sins of the world then, yours and mine, and He saw, too, that many, even after He had died for them, would not love Him, but would sin and grieve Him to the very end.

He taught us in this agony of prayer how we ought to pray to God to be spared a trial, but at the same time to say, no matter how much it hurts us, "God's will be done."

After these prayers Jesus went again to the disciples and awoke them, and said, "Rise. Let us go. Behold, he is at hand who will betray me."

Judas Betrays Jesus

When they had gone a little way, they met a great crowd of people and soldiers, and Judas was with them.

Judas had told the soldiers that the man he would kiss would be Jesus, and to take that man.

So Judas went up to Jesus, and said, "Hail, Master" and kissed Him. Jesus said to him, "Judas, do you betray the Son of Man with a kiss?" The soldiers then went to take Jesus, but Peter took out his sword and cut off the ear of one of them. Jesus told Peter to put away his sword, and touching the man's ear, He healed it, and gave Himself up quietly to the soldiers.

When the disciples saw that Jesus was taken, they ran away; Peter and John remained.

Jesus Before the High Priest

The crowd led Jesus to the house of a ruler named Annas, who asked Jesus many questions. Jesus answered that Annas should ask the people who had heard Him preach, as He had never taught in secret. For saying this, one of Annas's servants gave Jesus a slap.

Peter Denies Jesus

When Jesus was in the house of Annas, Peter was outside in the courtyard, where there was a fire burning, for it was cold; and about him were many people — soldiers and servants.

While Peter stood at the fire, very sad,
a servant woman came to warm herself also
and said, "This man was with Him." But
Peter said, "Woman, I do not know Him."

After a little while, a man said, "You also
are one of them." But Peter said, "I am not."

And again, in an hour, another man said,
"Truly this man was also with Him." Then

Peter again, with many strong words, said, "I do not know what you say."

Just as he spoke, the rooster crowed three times. Jesus passed through the court of Caiaphas, another ruler, to whom Annas had sent Him and He turned and looked at Peter.

Peter then remembered what Jesus had said: that he would deny Him three times before the rooster crowed. Going out, Peter wept bitterly.

The men who held Jesus struck Him cruelly, jeering at Him and crying out, "Say who it is that has struck You," but Jesus remained silent.

Caiaphas

When He was before Caiaphas, Jesus was asked if He was "the Christ, the Son of the blessed God."

Jesus answered, "I am."

Caiaphas did not believe this.

He said it was a wicked thing for Jesus to say, and he gave Jesus up into the hands of the people, to be taken the next day to the ruler, Pilate.

Pilate

Jesus was brought by the people to Pilate, who asked what He had done; and when Jesus had answered, he said, "I find no fault in the man." But the people only cried out all the more that Jesus was a disturber.

Now, it was a feast day, and it was the custom on those days, as an act of mercy, to release some man who was imprisoned for his crimes. So Pilate, who wished to make peace with the people, and perhaps get the release of Jesus, said to them, "There is in prison a man named Barabbas, who is a murderer. Shall I release him to you, or shall I release Jesus?"

The people said, "Let us have Barabbas, and crucify Jesus." But Pilate said to them, "Why? What evil has He done?" But they cried out the more, "Crucify Him!" So Pilate released Barabbas and gave Jesus up to them.

The Scourging

Pilate thought that if he made Jesus suffer, the people's hearts would be touched and he could save Him. So he had Jesus scourged,

which means whipped or flogged. But such a painful flogging! You cannot imagine it!

The Crowning with Thorns

After that dreadful scourging, an old purple robe was put upon Jesus, a reed in His hand, and on His head a crown of thorns.

They made Jesus a mock king.

Coming up to Him, they mocked Him and, bending down before Him, said, "Hail, King of the Jews." Then they spat at Him and struck Him, pressing the thorns deep into His head by their blows.

How it must have hurt Jesus! How He suffered for those naughty thoughts we have sometimes! Often when you are asked why you have done a naughty thing, you will say, "I don't know. It came into my head."

When these things come into your head, think for a moment of the crown of thorns on the head of Jesus, and you will not do wrong.

Pilate

When Pilate saw what a dreadful state Jesus was in after all this cruel work, he thought that if he would show Jesus to the people, they would have pity. So he led Jesus out on a balcony and said to the people, "Behold the man!"

But they had no pity and shouted, "Crucify Him." Pilate saw that it was no use to try to save Jesus, but he was afraid to lose the favor of the people, and he said to them, "He is a just man."

Then he called for a basin and washed his hands before the people, to show that his hands were clean of the death of Jesus. And he said to them, "I am innocent of the blood of this just man."

And the people cried out, "His blood be upon us and upon our children." Pilate then said Jesus was to die and gave Him up to the crowd.

The Way of the Cross

At that time it was the custom to crucify people who were to be killed for great crimes. That is, they nailed and tied a person to a cross and left him hanging there until he died.

Jesus, then, all weak and torn and bleeding, was led out of Pilate's house by the people, and they made Him carry on His shoulders the Cross on which He was to die.

What a sad sight it must have been for Mary, His mother, and His disciples and

friends to see! Even the other women and
children cried for very pity when they saw
Jesus bending under the weight of the great
Cross He was carrying.

Jesus turned to these poor women and said,
"Daughters of Jerusalem, do not weep for me,
but weep for yourselves and for your children."

The place to which Jesus had to carry His Cross was called Calvary. It was where criminals were put to death. With Jesus were two wicked men who were also going to Calvary to be put to death.

Jesus was so weak when He was carrying His Cross that He fell down three times. At last He could carry it no further, and the soldiers made a man named Simon, who was passing by, carry the Cross the rest of the way.

Jesus Is Nailed to the Cross

When they arrived at Calvary, the Cross was put on the ground, and the soldiers took Jesus and stripped off His clothes. Then Jesus was laid upon the Cross, and men came with a hammer and three nails.

They roughly pulled our Savior's hand to one side of the Cross and drove the large nail through it, fastening it to the Cross; they did the same with the other hand. His feet were crossed over each other, and one nail was driven through both, and so Jesus was fastened to the Cross. The nails were large, to bear the weight.

What pain it must have been! Imagine each blow of the hammer driving the nail through the flesh! How sick Mary must have felt at the dreadful sound of the hammer! We cannot even imagine the pain of Jesus. We would scream and cry out if a pin were put through our hand; but Jesus was quite silent.

On the Cross

Have you ever seen men put a large stone or pillar or pole into the ground? They first dig a deep hole; then they tie ropes to the pole and place one end of the pole just by the hole. Then they go a good many feet off and pull on these ropes. The pole slowly rises up and then goes into the hole with a sudden jerk.

That is how the Cross to which Jesus was nailed was jerked into the hole. That jerk must have been a terrible agony. The wounds in His hands and feet must have been torn larger by it and must have bled more.

At the foot of the Cross stood Mary and John. You remember that Simeon had told Mary, long ago, that a sword of sorrow would pierce her heart; and what sorrow could be greater than to see a good, tender Son suffer such pain at the hands of cruel men?

When Jesus was hanging there in this cruel state, the crowd mocked Him, saying, "He saved others. Let Him save Himself if He is Christ."

And the soldiers also mocked Him, saying, "If You are the King of the Jews, save Yourself." And they wrote in Latin, on the top of His Cross, in scorn, these words: "This is the King of the Jews." (That is what the "I.N.R.I." means on the crucifixes you see: "Jesus of Nazareth, King of the Jews.")

But Jesus still loved and prayed for these wicked men, saying, "Father, forgive them, for they know not what they do."

The Thieves

The two bad men, who were thieves, or robbers, were also crucified with Jesus, being put at each side of Him. One of these robbers mocked Jesus too, saying, "If You are Christ, save Yourself and us."

But the other robber said to him in rebuke, "We suffer justly, for we receive the due reward of our deeds; but this man has done no evil."

And he said to Jesus, "Lord, remember me when You go to heaven." And Jesus said to him, "Amen, I say to you, this day you shall be with me in paradise" (heaven).

Jesus Speaks to Mary

When Jesus saw Mary standing with John at the foot of His Cross, He said to Mary, "Woman, behold your son," and to John, "Behold your mother." And from that hour the disciple took her as his own mother. Jesus, in saying this, gave Mary to us all as our mother.

Jesus Dies

Jesus had now been hanging in torture on the cross for three hours. He was in such pain of body and soul that He called out, "My God, my God, why have You abandoned me?"

He then said, "I thirst." A soldier who was near dipped a sponge in vinegar and, putting it on a spear, lifted it up to Jesus, who, when

He had moistened His lips, cried out with a loud voice, "It is finished," and then with a great cry of prayer — "Father, into Your hands I commend my spirit" — He bowed His head and died.

The soldiers were filled with fear and cried out, "Indeed, this was the Son of God" — for the earth trembled, the rocks split, the sun was darkened, the graves opened, and the dead rose.

The people went back to Jerusalem full of fear. Later a soldier pierced the side of Jesus with a spear, and blood and water came out of the wound.

Jesus Is Put in the Tomb

Joseph, a rich man and a ruler, who believed in secret in Jesus, went at night to Pilate, and asked leave to take the body of Jesus and bury it. Pilate gave him leave. So Joseph and his friends took down the body of Jesus from the Cross, wrapped it in white cloths and sweet spices, and put it in a tomb. The tomb was a new one, cut out of rock, and had a great stone to close it up. Joseph had intended it for his own body when he died.

The rulers knew that Jesus had said He would rise again from the dead in three days, so they sent a guard of soldiers to watch the tomb, for they said the disciples would steal away the body and say He had risen, and so people would believe. So Pilate put his great seal on the tomb.

The Resurrection

The third day had now come. It was the early morning, and the soldiers were at watch, when all at once the earth shook, and an angel came to the tomb and rolled back the stone, and Jesus came out and showed Himself to the soldiers, all glorious and beautiful. His face shone like the sun, and the soldiers, afraid, ran away and told the rulers.

The rulers, who were now afraid that the crowds would believe, gave the soldiers a great sum of money and told them to say that the disciples had stolen the body. This the Jews believed.

Mary Magdalene and other women came
that same morning to the tomb with spices.
On their way they asked one another how they
would roll away the large stone from the door
of the tomb, to put in their spices. But when
they arrived, they found the stone removed
and the body of Jesus gone.

Mary Magdalene left at once to tell the Apostles that the body of Jesus was gone. The other women looked into the tomb, for they saw a bright light, and there sat an angel, who said to them, "Be not afraid. You seek Jesus of Nazareth, who was crucified. He is risen; He is not here. Behold the place where they laid Him. But go tell His disciples and Peter, that He goes before you into Galilee. There you shall see Him, as He told you."

Jesus Appears to Mary Magdalene

Mary Magdalene ran and told Peter and the other disciple whom Jesus loved. "They have taken away the Lord out of the tomb, and we do not know where they have laid Him."

Peter and John ran to the tomb, but they could find nobody, and they returned to their homes.

Mary Magdalene stayed at the tomb weeping, and stooping down and looking into the tomb, she saw two angels dressed in white, and they said to her, "Woman, why do you weep?"

She said to them, "Because they have taken away my Lord, and I do not know where they have laid Him." When she turned around, she saw a man standing there; she thought he was the gardener, and she said to Him, "Sir, if you have taken Him hence, tell me where you have laid Him, and I will take Him away."

Jesus (for it was Jesus) said to her, "Mary." Turning to Him, she said, "Rabboni" (Master). Jesus then told her to go and tell His Apostles, and say to them, "I ascend to my Father and your Father, to my God and your God." And Mary did as she was told.

Jesus Appears to His Apostles

That day the Apostles were in a room with the door locked, afraid of the people, when Jesus came in — they did not know how — and said to them, "Peace be to you." When He had said this, He showed them His hands and His side; and they were glad to see Him.

Thomas, who was one of the disciples, was not present when Jesus was there, and on his return the other disciples said to him, "We have seen the Lord!" But he said to them, "Unless I see in His hands the print of the nails, and put my finger into the place of the nails, and put my hand into His side, I will not believe."

When eight days were passed, the disciples were again in the same room, and Thomas was with them. Jesus came, even though the door was locked, and stood in the midst and said, "Peace be to you."

Then He said to Thomas, "Put in your finger here, and see my hands; and bring your hand and put it into my side; and be not faithless, but believing."

Thomas answered and said to Him, "My Lord and my God!" Jesus said to him, "Because you have seen me, Thomas, you have believed. Blessed are they who have not seen and have believed."

Peter

Jesus came another time to His disciples, and this time He asked Peter three times if he loved Him. And Peter each time said to Him, "Yes, Lord, You know that I love You." And each time he said it, Jesus told him, "Feed my lambs," and the last time, "Feed my sheep."

In these words Jesus meant to show that Peter was the chief of the Apostles; the lambs show that we are children of the Church, and the sheep are the priests.

Ever since Jesus told Peter, "Feed my lambs; feed my sheep," the Church has always had one man who succeeds Peter, and he is known as the Pope. We are the children (the lambs), and the priests (the sheep) teach us.

But the Pope (Peter) guides us all — lambs and sheep, people and priests.

The Promise of the Holy Spirit

Jesus had often shown Himself to His disciples, and on one occasion when He came to them, He breathed on them and said to them, "Receive the Holy Spirit; whose sins you shall forgive, they are forgiven them, and whose sins you shall retain, they are retained."

In saying this, Jesus gave power to His Apostles and to His priests to forgive our sins if we confess them and are sorry for them. He taught them many things they had not known before.

Forty days after Jesus had left the tomb and risen from the dead, He came again to the disciples and told them to stay in Jerusalem for some days, for He was about to leave them, but would send the Holy Spirit to comfort them.

The Ascension

After this Jesus went with His Apostles to Mount Olivet.

There He blessed them, and as He was blessing them, the wonder and power of God were shown.

Slowly, and in a bright light, Jesus was lifted from the ground and was raised up into the skies — into heaven — as they strained their eyes to look after Him.

They were sorry to see Jesus go from them, and they remained in awe and wonder, looking up where Jesus had gone.

At last two angels in white garments spoke to the Apostles and told them, "This Jesus, whom you have seen ascending into heaven, shall come again."

The Apostles praised God and went back into Jerusalem as our Lord had commanded, to wait for the Holy Spirit.

Conclusion

You have now read, dear children, most of the stories of the Old and New Testament. Read them often, and when you are older, you will never forget that these stories were told for your good, and in the hope that the seed sown in childhood's years may produce fruit even to the end of your days.

Sophia Institute Press®

Sophia Institute® is a nonprofit institution that seeks to restore man's knowledge of eternal truth, including man's knowledge of his own nature, his relation to other persons, and his relation to God. Sophia Institute Press® serves this end in numerous ways: it publishes translations of foreign works to make them accessible for the first time to English-speaking readers; it brings out-of-print books back into print; and it publishes important new books that fulfill the ideals of Sophia Institute®. These books afford readers a rich source of the enduring wisdom of mankind.

Sophia Institute Press® makes these high-quality books available to the general public by using advanced technology and by soliciting donations to subsidize its general publishing costs. Your generosity can help Sophia Institute Press® to provide the public with editions of works containing the enduring wisdom of the ages. Please send your tax-deductible contribution to the address below. We also welcome your questions, comments, and suggestions.

For your free catalog, call:
Toll-free: 1-800-888-9344
or write:
Sophia Institute Press®
Box 5284, Manchester, NH 03108
or visit our website:
www.sophiainstitute.com

Sophia Institute® is a tax-exempt institution as defined by the Internal Revenue Code, Section 501(c)(3). Tax I.D. 22-2548708.